Contents

Introduction...5

Neighbourhoods..6

El Born..8

El Barri Gòtic 28

El Raval...34

Poblenou & Barceloneta..44

L'Eixample..62

Gràcia...82

Sant Antoni & Montjuïc...92

Essentials..106

Index...108

Metro Map...112

Credits...114

About the Series...116

Barcelona

—Welcome to Analogue Barcelona

Set amid the stunning natural beauty of the Mediterranean coast, Barcelona is at once Europe's casual beachside metropolis and the sophisticated capital of industrious and design-conscious Catalonia. During the summer months, the city's sandy urban beaches resemble a European take on Miami or Venice Beach. Leafier neighbourhoods further uphill are the heartland of Catalan architecture and cuisine.

Barcelona thrived as a major entrepôt under the Crown of Aragon until its demise in 1716. On 11 September 1714, Barcelona capitulated, uniting Spain and abolishing Catalan autonomy. During the Spanish Civil War, liberal Catalonia backed the losing Republican side and consequently faced decades of cultural suppression under Franco's dictatorship. Barcelona splashed back onto the global scene with the 1992 Olympics, showcasing its extensively revitalised seafront.

Today, Barcelona's picture perfect urbanity, meticulously orchestrated by the *Generalitat* bureaucracy, combines a liberal mind set with a Mediterranean lifestyle. In recent years, the city has simultaneously seen a strong resurgence of Catalan culture and a diverse influx of immigrants from across the world. Its new diversity is perhaps best displayed in the Born's wealth of outdoor cafés, delightful restaurants and independent boutiques. The city's avant-garde has shifted into the formerly industrial Poblenou, while the grand Eixample is home to Gaudí inspired architecture and the high-end establishments of great Catalan chefs.

We've endeavoured to gather the best of what this wonderful city has to offer, with photography and maps throughout. Enjoy!

Neighbourhoods

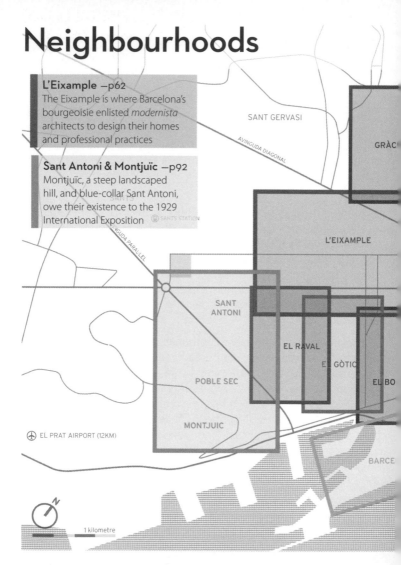

L'Eixample —p62
The Eixample is where Barcelona's bourgeoisie enlisted *modernista* architects to design their homes and professional practices

Sant Antoni & Montjuïc —p92
Montjuïc, a steep landscaped hill, and blue-collar Sant Antoni, owe their existence to the 1929 International Exposition

SANT GERVASI

AVINGUDA DIAGONAL

GRÀCIA

SANTS

SANTS STATION

L'EIXAMPLE

AVINGUDA PARAL·LEL

SANT ANTONI

EL RAVAL

EL GÒTIC

EL BO

POBLE SEC

MONTJUIC

EL BARCE

EL PRAT AIRPORT (12KM)

N

1 kilometre

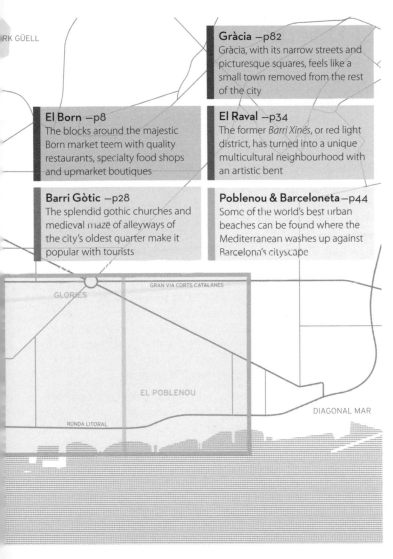

RK GÜELL

Gràcia —p82
Gràcia, with its narrow streets and picturesque squares, feels like a small town removed from the rest of the city

El Born —p8
The blocks around the majestic Born market teem with quality restaurants, specialty food shops and upmarket boutiques

El Raval —p34
The former *Barri Xinés*, or red light district, has turned into a unique multicultural neighbourhood with an artistic bent

Barri Gòtic —p28
The splendid gothic churches and medieval maze of alleyways of the city's oldest quarter make it popular with tourists

Poblenou & Barceloneta—p44
Some of the world's best urban beaches can be found where the Mediterranean washes up against Barcelona's cityscape

GLÒRIES

GRAN VIA CORTS CATALANES

EL POBLENOU

DIAGONAL MAR

RONDA LITORAL

El Born

—Bijou Boutiques and Meandering Alleys

Barcelona's second oldest part after the Barri Gotic (p28), the Born consists of three distinct areas: Sant Pere, Santa Caterina and La Ribera. Technically speaking, the "Born" only refers to the blocks around the 19th century Born market, Barcelona's first inner city neighborhood to regenerate. Today, it is decidedly upmarket with a distinct creative bent.

The origins of Sant Pere, Santa Catarina and La Ribera can be traced back to the eleventh century, when Barcelona outgrew its Roman walls. At its lower fringes near the sea, La Ribera developed distinct maritime traditions, of which the Santa Maria del Mar church is a dazzling reminder. In the early 18th century, large swathes of this area were razed by Philip V of Spain to make way for an extensive fortress designed to maintain control over Barcelona. Much loathed by residents, the structure was replaced by the Parc de la Ciutadella (p13) in the late 19th century. Subsequent efforts were made to update the area's medieval cityscape—Carrer Princesa and the magnificent Mercat del Born (pictured on the right), now a cultural centre, opened—but it remained by and large a crowded and squalid place until well into the mid-20th century.

Today, the Born's classical buildings and narrow alleys teem with quality restaurants, specialty food shops and upmarket boutiques. Some of this lustre has spilled over into less well-off Sant Pere and Santa Catarina, which have a more mixed make-up of locals, immigrants and euro-expats. The adjacent Parc de la Ciutadella, with its lush Mediterranean vegetation, is the largest inner city park in Barcelona and also home to Barcelona's zoo.

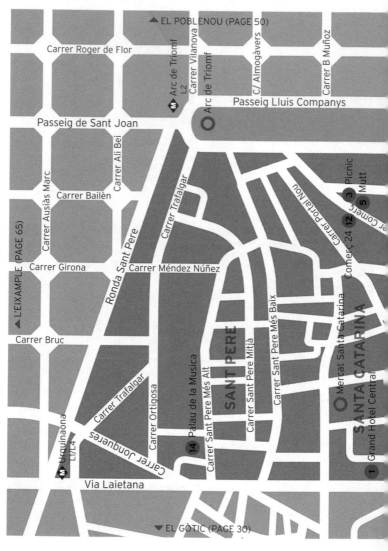

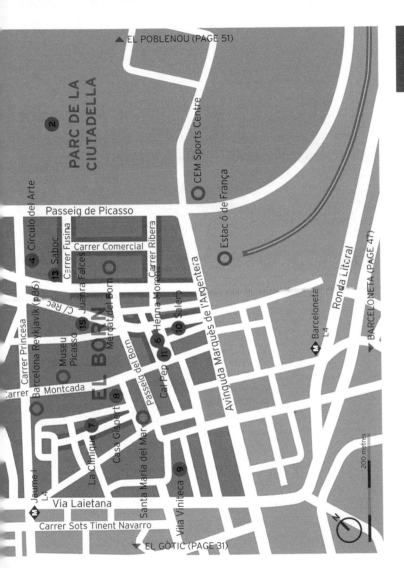

▲ EL POBLENOU (PAGE 51)

PARC DE LA CIUTADELLA

2

○ CEM Sports Centre

○ Estac ó de França

Circulo de Arte

Passeig de Picasso

4 ○

Saboc

13

Carrer Comercial

Carrer Fusina

Carrer Falces

Juerra

Carrer Ribera

Henna Morena

Carrer Princesa

Barcelona Revkjavik (p86)

C/ Rec

15

Mercat del Born

EL BORN

6 **11**

Henna Morena

10 Salero

Museu Picasso

Carrer Montcada

8

Passeig del Born

Cal Pep

Avinguda Marquès de l'Argentera

○

M Barceloneta
L4

Ronda Litoral

▶ BARCELONETA (PAGE 47)

Carrer

7 La Clinique

Casa Gispert

Santa Maria del Mar

Jaume I
L4

Vila Viniteca

9

Via Laietana

Carrer Sots Tinent Navarro

▼ EL GÒTIC (PAGE 31)

200 metres

N

Old Town Grand Hotel

Grand Hotel Central

Via Laietana, 30
+34 932 95 79 00
grandhotelcentral.com
◆ Jaume I L4
Doubles from €231/night incl. tax

The Grand Hotel Central offers luxurious accommodation in an urbane setting. Centrally located on the Via Laietana, the dividing line between the Born and the Gòtic, the hotel boasts a gorgeous rooftop bar and infinity pool with breathtaking views over the city. Rooms are tastefully appointed in soft tones and exude elegant contemporary flair.

Gorgeous Park

Parc de la Ciutadella

2 between Passeig de Pujades and Passeig de Picasso

◈ Arc de Triomf **L1** , Barceloneta **L4** , Wellington ↘

Public access.

The largest green space in central Barcelona, the park's 30 hectares of lush Mediterranean vegetation boast a grandiose water cascade loosely modelled after Rome's Trevi Fountain, a boating lake, orange groves and conservatories, and scores of parrots. The park was created in the mid 19th century on the site of Barcelona's former citadel and was the site of the 1888 Barcelona World Fair, to which the nearby Moorish style Arc de Triomf was the entrance gate. For a refreshing dip during the summer months, head to the park-side CEM sports centre (map p11) to lounge at its attractive rooftop pool.

Brunch by the Park

Picnic

③ Carrer de Comerç, 1
+34 935 11 66 61
picnic-restaurant.com

◈ Arc de Triomf **L1**

Open daily. Lunch Mon-Fri 1pm-4pm. Dinner Tue-Sat 8pm-12.30am (Cocktails until 2am). Brunch Sat/Sun 11.30am-5pm.

Painted in white and light blue tones, Picnic's friendly but sophisticated vibe brings brunch to the Born. If you're dropping by slightly later, opt for dinner at the bar or an evening cocktail on the terrace. Chef and co-owner Jaime Riesco spins fresh seasonal produce into dishes inspired by the Chilean, American and Australian provenances of the restaurant's creators. And for an excellent post-Picnic stroll amid palm trees and green parakeets, head to nearby Ciutadella Park (p13).

Art Club & Gallery

Círculo del Arte

④ Carrer Princesa, 52
+34 932 68 88 20
circulodelarte.com

◈ Jaume I L4
Closed Sun. Open Mon-Fri 10am-7pm; Sat 10am-2pm, 4pm-8pm (except August).
Free admission

In 1994, a group of artists, publishers and gallerists of international renown established this arts club to provide original visual artwork and to promote the collection of high quality prints. At its spacious Born headquarters the Círculo del Arte shows works by contemporary artists, as well as hosting cultural events and selling art books. Recent exhibitions have included *Steidlville*, an excellent retrospective of the Steidl publishing house.

Design Literature

Mutt

5 Carrer Comerç 15
+34 931 92 44 38
mutt.es

◆ Arc de Triomf **L1**
Closed Sun. Open Mon-Sat 11am-2pm, 4pm-8pm.

Flanked by elegant 19th century apartment blocks, Mutt's inspiring Carrer del Comerç surroundings reflect the heterogeneous content of its walls and shelves. At once a design-focused bookshop and art gallery, this is the place to come for an afternoon browse through a top rate selection of art, architecture and design related publications. A floor-to-ceiling glass front makes for sundrenched viewing of the contemporary art on offer.

Essence of the Med

Henna Morena

6 Carrer Esparteria, 12
+34 933 151 191
hennamorena.com
◆ Jaume I **L4** , Barceloneta **L4**
Closed Sun. Open Mon 4:30pm-
8:30pm, Tue-Sat 11am-8:30pm.

For a true flavour of the Mediterranean in a spa-like setting, head to Henna Morena. This shop purveys an organic range of shampoos, essential oils and henna based hair care products made from locally sourced botanicals, in addition to pure Karité Shea butter bars, individually wrapped in gorgeous fabric from Burkina Faso. After some retail therapy, recline in the back room's comfy chairs while Henna based treatments are applied to your hair.

Vintage Specs

La Clinique

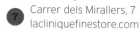 Carrer dels Mirallers, 7
lacliniquefinestore.com

◈ Jaume I L4

Closed Sun. Open Mon-Sat 11.30am-
3pm, 4.30pm-8.30pm.

La Clinique is a repository of Gallic *branché* hidden deep inside one of the Born's meandering back alleys. The azure tiled treasure trove of chic refurbished vintage sunglasses, shoes, accessories, stationary, vinyl and urban wear makes for a shopping frenzy, staged with an outer space-like whimsy. An ode to the beauty of classic design.

Roasted Nuts and Dried Fruits

Casa Gispert

8 Carrer Sombrerers, 23
+34 933 19 75 35
casagispert.com

◆ Jaume I **L4**

Closed Sun/Mon. Open Tue-Fri
9.30am-2pm, 4pm-8.30pm; Sat
10am-2pm, 5pm-8.30pm.

Once you've tasted a Casa Gispert *almendra tostada*, no nut will ever be its equal. Delve into the magical microcosm of this historical shop and discover some of Barcelona's best produce. Woven baskets overflow with pistachios, dates, chocolates and coffee beans, while the shop's walls are lined with extra virgin olive oils and a mesmerising assortment of spices that transport you back to 1851, when it first opened.

Premier Wine Shop

Vila Viniteca

 Carrer Agullers, 7
+34 902 32 77 77

vilaviniteca.es

◈ Jaume I **L4**

Closed Sun. Open Mon-Sat 8.30am-8.30pm; July/August Sat 8.30am-2.30pm.

An outstanding wine retailer with a strong focus on Spain and France, Vila Viniteca is the place to go if you're looking for an excellent bottle and some sound, personalised oenological counselling. Contemplate the floor to ceiling array of *riberas*, *riojas*, *priorats* and *jerez* or allow the staff to guide you on a whirlwind tour through your favourite wine region. The shop regularly hosts *catas* (wine tastings) and if you feel the need to nibble on something with your *cava*, Vila has a sister delicatessen across the street.

Global Tides

Salero

10 Carrer Rec, 60
+34 933 19 80 22
restaurantesalero.com
◈ Barceloneta **L4**, Jaume I **L4**
Open Mon-Sun 1pm-4pm, 8.30pm-midnight.

Subtle but elegant, white-washed Salero brings the seafaring tradition of the old La Ribera and its global influences to the table. Fresh locally sourced produce is used to assemble a panoply of globally inspired dishes, a tribute to Barcelona's cosmopolitan nature. Feast on lamb tagine or an Asian-style sepia wok with a refreshing glass of *albariño* while observing the shoppers lining Carrer Rec outside.

Born Stalwart

Cal Pep

11 Carrer Rec, 60
+34 933 19 80 22
restaurantesalero.com

◆ Barceloneta **L4** , Jaume I **L4**
Closed Sun. Lunch Tue-Sat 1pm-
3.45pm. Dinner Mon-Fri 7.30pm-
11.30pm. Closed last three weeks of
August.

Cal Pep delivers wildly inventive Catalan cuisine in the form of seventy delectable tapas. While the setting and décor are traditional, Pep's repertoire is versatile and contemporary. Grab lunch along the buzzing front-room bar or reserve a table in the more spacious back room. Invigorate with an Atomic Omelet and Crunchy Pasta with Mushrooms and Prawn Tails before moving onto the Born's backstreets for some serious shopping.

The Catalan Touch

Comerç 24

12 Carrer Comerç, 24
+34 933 19 21 02
comerc24.com
◆ Arc de Triomf **L1**
Closed Sun/Mon. Open Tue-Sat
1.30pm-3.30pm, 8.30pm-11pm.

Famed Catalan restaurateur Carles Abellan's first restaurant, Comerç 24 is perhaps the most hip of Barcelona's "Great Catalan Chef" dining establishments. While in his twenties, Abellan trained under Ferran Adrià at El Bulli, subsequently moving on to managing other Adrià projects before starting his own venture. The results are predictably outstanding—a classic Mediterranean menu meets the best of world cuisine, with cutting edge Catalan culinary craft, in a classy, unpretentious setting.

Temperature Cuisine

Saboc

 Carrer de la Fusina, 3
+34 932 68 30 80

saboc.es

◈ Jaume I L4

Open daily. Lunch 1pm-4pm; Dinner 8pm-11.30pm. Coffee & Tea 4pm-8pm.

Saboc is a cosmopolitan restaurant specializing in globally inspired small plates prepared at specific temperatures. Dishes come in one of four styles: raw, low-temperature, baked and grilled, and the emphasis is on tasting a range of complementary flavours across the spectrum of cooking methods, as if the meal were a wine tasting. The restaurant occupies a prime spot across the street from the recently remodeled Mercat del Born, now a cultural centre, and within eyeshot of the area's wealth of avant-garde boutiques.

Modernista Music

Palau de la Musica

14 Carrer Palau de la Musica, 4-6
+34 902 44 28 82
palaumusica.cat

◈ Urquinaona **L1 L4**,
Catalunya **L1 L3 L6 L7**
Regular performances. Refer to
website for program.

The jewel in the crown of
Barcelona's manifold *palaus*, the
Palau de la Musica is a gorgeous
modernista auditorium. An
architectural treasure with excellent
acoustics, this is the place to go
if you're craving live classical, jazz
or chamber music in enchanting
surroundings. To fully take in the
setting, pre-concert *canapés* and
cava are de rigueur.

Mahogany and Ice

Juanra Falces

 Carrer del Rec, 24
+34 933 101 027

◈ Jaume I L4

Open daily. Sun-Mon 10pm-3am; Tue-Sat 8pm-3am.

Sit around the mahogany bar of this Born institution and enjoy classic cocktails served by discrete, knowledgeable mixologists. Juanra Falces, formerly known as Gimlet, is bang in the centre of one of the neighbourhood's most vibrant commercial stretches, yet step inside and the soft jazz and gentle clinking of ice will transport you worlds away. The ideal spot to pamper yourself after those long hours of *cultura y compras*.

El Barri Gòtic

—Medieval Maze

The Barri Gòtic, the "gothic quarter", is the oldest part of Barcelona and its political and administrative centre. It is separated from the Born (p8) by neoclassical Via Laietana, an early 20th century incursion, and from the Raval (p34) by the popular Ramblas. Most of the Gòtic is defined by small streets lined with narrow dwellings interspersed with mansions and splendid gothic churches, among them Barcelona Cathedral and Santa Maria del Pi.

At the Gòtic's core lie the ruins of the Roman settlement of *Barcino*, though most of the area's architecture today dates from the 14th and 15th centuries, the heyday of Barcelona's maritime power. The centre of the former Roman city is today's Plaça Saint Jaume; still the focal point of political power and the site of both Barcelona's town hall and the *Generalitat*, the government of Catalonia. On the southern edge of Plaça Saint Jaume is the entrance to the Call, the city's medieval Jewish quarter. An entrancing world unto itself, the Call is linked to the rest of the Gòtic through a limited number of narrow passageways. Its charming alleyways, dotted with distinct boutiques and cafés, provide a calm refuge from the frenzy of the surrounding streets.

In the 19th century efforts were made to provide public space in the crowded Old Town, notably the atmospheric Plaça Reial, a Spanish-style plaza just off the Ramblas. Formerly populated by wealthy residents, the square has, like much of the neighbourhood, largely given in to its popularity with tourists. Today, the Gòtic's upper reaches are pedestrianised and dominated by a predictable set of retail brands. However, the narrow streets near the port still offer some of the magic of wandering through the maze of a medieval city.

- ▲ EL BORN (PAGE 10)

Urquinaona
L1/L4

Carrer Jonqueres

Via Laietana

1 Koy Shunka

Carrer Comtal

◄ L'EIXAMPLE (PAGE 65)

Catalunya
L1/L3/L6/L7

Portal de l'Àngel

PLAÇA
CATALUNYA

Carrer Santa Anna

Carrer Canuda

Carrer Duc

Ronda Universitat

Carrer Bergara

Carrer Pelai

La Rambla

Carrer Tallers

Carrer d'Elisabets

Carrer Doctor Dou

Fortuny

Carrer Carme

Gardunya

rusalem

▼ EL RAVAL (PAGE 36)

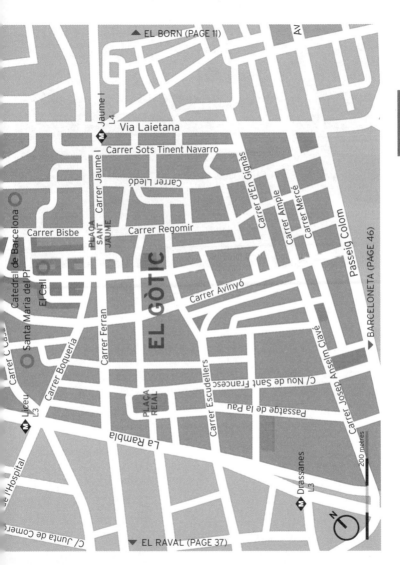

▲ EL BORN (PAGE 11)

Via Laietana

Carrer Sots Tinent Navarro

Carrer Lledó

Carrer d'En Gignàs

Carrer Ample

Carrer Mercé

Passeig Colom

► BARCELONETA (PAGE 46)

Carrer Bisbe

Carrer Regomir

PLAÇA SANT JAUME

Catedral de Barcelona

Santa Maria del Pi

El Call

EL GÒTIC

Carrer Avinyó

Carrer Josep Anselm Clavé

Carrer Ferran

Carrer Boqueria

Carrer Escudellers

C/ Nou de Sant Francesc

Passatge de la Pau

PLAÇA REIAL

La Rambla

Liceu L3

i l'Hospital

Drassanes L3

C/ Junta de Comerç

▼ EL RAVAL (PAGE 37)

Jaume I L4

Carrer Jaume I

200 metres

N

Premier Sushi

Koy Shunka

① Carrer Copons, 7
+34 934 12 79 39

koyshunka.com

◆ Urquinaona L1 L4,
Catalunya L1 L3 L6 L7
Closed Mon. Lunch Tue-Sun 1.30pm-3pm. Dinner Tue-Sat 8.30pm-11pm.

Koy Shunka, "intense seasonal aroma" in Japanese, is a refined Michelin starred Japanese restaurant. Chef Hideki Matsuhisa moved to Barcelona in 1997 when he opened his first, casual venue, Shunka, a few streets down. Koy Shunka, a decidedly more upscale affair, followed suit, opening in 2008. The result is an uncompromising, seasonally driven menu, where *sashimi* and *wagyu* melt in the mouth in a modern and sophisticated setting.

El Raval

—Avant-garde Hotbed

The third of Barcelona's three Old Town neighbourhoods, the Raval has had a dubious reputation for much of its history. Recent immigrants attracted by cheap rents mixed with urbane spillovers from the Ramblas and the famous Boqueria market (p39) have created a unique multicultural neighborhood with an artistic bent.

The diamond shaped Raval came into being in the 15th century when Barcelona's city walls were expanded from today's Ramblas to include empty tracts of land to the west of the city. Sparsely populated yet safely located inside the city walls and close to the port, the Raval became the logical site for less desirable activities, and from the 18th century, factories and working class housing. Revolts and epidemics in the crowded Old Town played an important part in the decision to tear down the city walls in 1859 and create the Eixample (p62). Most industrial activity moved to more spacious territory outside the former city walls, leaving the Raval predominantly residential. Its overcrowded streets, proximity to the port and plethora of bars, theatres and brothels soon conferred it the nickname *el Barri Xinès*, the Chinese quarter.

Still infamous today, and quite seedy in its lower stretches towards the port, much effort has been made to rejuvenate the Raval and improve the lot of its residents, around half of whom are foreign born. Entire blocks have been razed to provide contemporary housing, and Barcelona's Center of Contemporary Art (CCCB, p40) and Museum of Contemporary Art (MACBA) opened in the 1990s. Its central location and relative affordability have also made it a fertile breeding ground for number of independent shops and restaurants, and the artistic types who populate them.

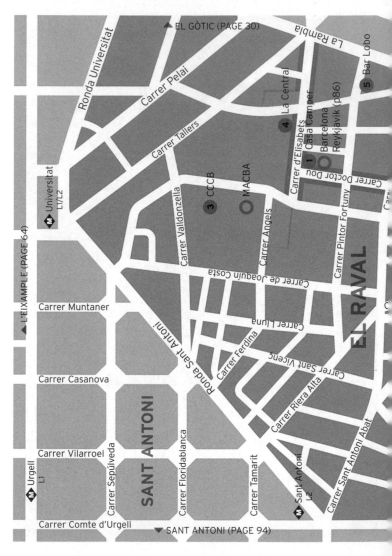

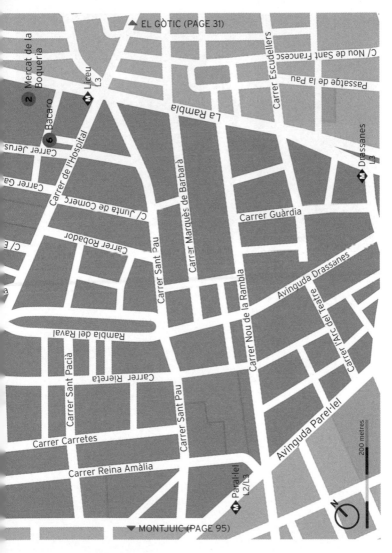

▲ EL GÒTIC (PAGE 31)

Mercat de la Boqueria ②

Bàcaro ⑥

Liceu M L3

La Rambla

Carrer Escudellers

C/ Nou de Sant Francesc

Passatge de la Pau

Carrer Jerus

Carrer de l'Hospital

Carrer Ga

C/ Junta de Comerç

Carrer Marquès de Barbarà

Carrer Guàrdia

Drassanes M L3

Carrer Robador

C/ E

Carrer Sant Pau

Rambla del Raval

Carrer Nou de la Rambla

Avinguda Drassanes

Carrer Sant Pacià

Carrer Riereta

Carrer l'Arc del Teatre

Carrer Sant Pau

Carrer Carretes

Avinguda Paral·lel

Carrer Reina Amàlia

Paral·lel M L2/L3

200 metres

▼ MONTJUIC (PAGE 95)

N

Hotel by Camper

Casa Camper

1 Carrer d'Elisabets, 11
+34 933 42 62 80
casacamper.com
◆ Universitat **L1 L2**, Liceu **L3**
Doubles from €215/night incl. tax

Much like the quality and comfort driven shoes produced by the same Mallorcan team, Casa Camper's obsession is simple luxury. Located on a creative stretch of the Raval, down the street from the CCCB (p40) and MACBA museums, Casa Camper offers a quirky oasis of respite from the neighbourhood's hustle. A decidedly local affair, the on-site restaurant, Michelin starred Dos Pallilos, is headed by former El Bulli chef de cuisine Albert Raurich, while the hotel's interior is the brainchild of Ferran Amat, of design emporium Vinçon (p74).

King of Markets

Mercat de la Boqueria

 La Rambla, 91
+34 933 18 25 84
boqueria.info
◆ Liceu ⬛
Closed Sun. Open Mon-Sat 8am-8.30pm.

A feast for the senses, La Boqueria is undoubtedly market-dense Barcelona's preeminent incarnation of the genre. Row upon row of colourful produce spills over its seemingly unending corridors, while patrons jostle against one another at its ebullient food stalls, cafés and shops. With origins dating back to fruit and vegetable merchants of the 1200s, the Market's present version, with its towering steel roof and labyrinthine passages, took root in the early 1900s and has been mesmerising generations since.

Exhibition Space

CCCB

 Carrer Montalegre, 5
+34 933 06 41 00
cccb.org
◆ Universitat **L1** **L2**,
Catalunya **L1** **L3** **L6** **L7**
Closed Mon. Open Tue-Sun 11am-
8pm. Admission €6.

With a mandate to explore the workings of the urban space and culture, the Centre de Cultura Contemporània de Barcelona's exhibitions provide in-depth access to unusual aspects of Barcelona's cityscape and social history. Recent exhibitions have included a captivating examination of the turn of the century entertainment district, Avenguda Paral·lel, and an exploration of Barcelona, Girona and Blanes through the lens of narrative work by Chilean author Roberto Bolaño, whose greatest fictional achievements were composed in these Catalan cities.

Bookshop Heaven

La Central

④ Carrer d'Elisabets, 6
+34 902 88 49 90
lacentral.com
◈ Catalunya L1 L3 L6 L7,
Universitat L1 L2
Closed Sun. Open Mon-Fri 9.30am-
9pm; Sat 10am-9pm.

Barcelona based institution La Central is a group of intellectually stimulating and aesthetically pleasing bookshops-cum-cultural centres. The Raval branch, in the area's artistic and multicultural core, is particularly conducive to an afternoon of relaxed browsing. Follow with an organic pastry from the local outpost of Barcelona Reykjavik (p86) down Carrer Elisabets. La Central's Eixample branch (see map p64) boasts an in-house café.

Casual Cuisine

Bar Lobo

5 Carrer Pintor Fortuny, 3
+34 934 81 53 46
grupotragaluz.com

◈ Catalunya **L1** **L3** **L6** **L7**, Liceu **L3**
Open daily. Sun-Wed 9am-midnight;
Thu-Sat 9am-2.30am.

Restaurant magnate Tragaluz's Raval outlet is a casual-chic restaurant and *bar de copas* spread over two floors, offering an antidote to the area's rough edges. The restaurant covers the breakfast to dinner crowd as well as those simply looking to enjoy a *café solo* (espresso) or a glass of *cava* while mulling over their print purchases from nearby La Central (p41)

Venetian Fare

Bacaro

 Carrer Jerusalem, 6
+34 695 79 60 66

◈ Liceu Ⓛ

Closed Sun. Lunch Mon-Sat 1pm-4pm. Dinner Mon-Sat 8.30pm-midnight.

One of the city's most authentic and convivial Italian restaurants is unsurprisingly squeezed in a rough and tumble corner behind the Boquería market (p39). Run by a trio of affable Venetians, Mauri, Alfredo and Pablo, Bacaro (wine bar in Venetian) delivers consistently excellent fare from the Veneto, accompanied by wines from the same region. The tiny restaurant draws a steady stream of Italian expats hungry for *bresaola* and *prosecco* on the Iberian side of the Med.

Poblenou & Barceloneta

—Maritime Traditions

Barcelona is famously endowed with some of the world's best urban beaches. Barceloneta uniquely combines the bustle of a historic city centre with a sandy Mediterranean beach. Up the coast, the Poblenou's warehouses have been taken over by creative types and its beaches provide a relaxing alternative to crowded Barceloneta.

Barceloneta, a maritime neighborhood through and through, dates back to the 18th century, when the sands off the port's breakwater were built up to accommodate those displaced by the construction of the Ciutadela fortification (see p13). Its elongated streets and narrow blocks became a hotspot for metallurgy and shipbuilding, and later light industries like carpentry and watchmaking. Despite its beachfront location, Barceloneta has maintained a distinct blue-collar character, now interspersed with holiday flats and restaurants catering to tourists. Opened in 1931, the Port Vell Aerial Tramway links Barceloneta with Montjuïc (p92) across the port.

The Poblenou was formerly a fishing village set amid reed-lined lagoons but morphed into the industrial centre of 19th century Spain, the "Catalan Manchester", when it was swallowed up by Barcelona. Deindustrialised and decayed, the transformation of the area began when underused workshops and rail tracks made way for the 1992 Olympic village and marina. Today, the area around the Port Olímpic with its twin towers and giant Frank Gehry fish sculpture has a distinct 1990s commercial character. The Poblenou's creative scene with galleries and cafés is centered on the Carrer Pujades. After the early 2000s development binge of Diagonal Mar, efforts are now centred on a technology and design led regeneration of the area around Glòries square and the Torre Agbar skyscraper.

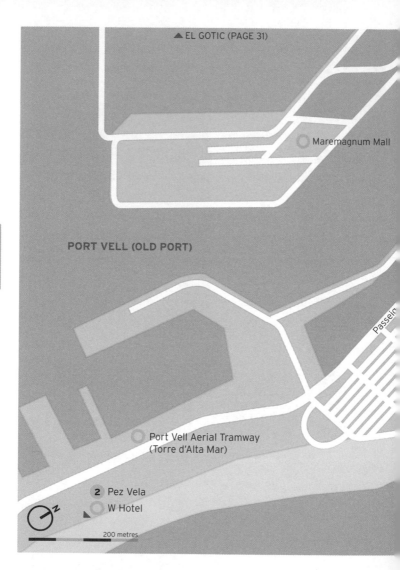

▲ EL GOTIC (PAGE 31)

Maremagnum Mall

PORT VELL (OLD PORT)

Passeig

Port Vell Aerial Tramway
(Torre d'Alta Mar)

2 Pez Vela

W Hotel

N

200 metres

▲ EL BORN (PAGE 11)
Ⓜ Barceloneta
L4

PARC DE LA CIUTADELLA

Carrer Doctor Aiguader

Carrer Balboa

Carrer Ginjbra

Ronda Litoral

Carrer Maquinista

Carrer l'Atlantida

Carrer Cermeño

Passeig Salvat Papasseit

e Barceló

▲ EL POBLENOU (PAGE 51)

BARCELONETA

er l'Almirall Cervera

Passeig Marítim de la B

① Sal Café

PLATJA BARCELONETA

Sea Salt and Salad
Sal Café

1 Passeig Marítim de la Barceloneta

+34 932 24 07 07

salcafe.com

◈ Barceloneta L4

Open daily noon-midnight (winter noon-5pm). Lunch 1pm-4pm. Dinner 8pm-11pm (winter Fri/Sat 8pm-10pm).

Sal Café is a beachside *xiringuito/* restaurant with a 70s lounge-style interior and a generous outdoor deck overlooking the Med. More laid-back than the surrounding restaurants but decidedly grown-up compared to the standard *xiringuito*, Sal offers light and delicious Mediterranean, Asian and Brazilian inspired fare. Salads are particularly fresh and crisp and pair perfectly with a refreshing *copa* of *vino blanco*.

Beachside Dining

Pez Vela

(2) Passeig del Mare Nostrum, 19-21
+34 932 216 317
grupotragaluz.com

◈ Barceloneta L4

Open daily. Lunch Mon-Fri 1pm-
3.45pm, Sat/Sun 1pm-4:30pm.
Dinner Mon-Thu 8pm-11.30pm, Fri/
Sat 8pm-12.30am.

For a taste of summer all year round, head to this breezy, contemporary *xiringuito*-style restaurant at the foot of the imposing sail-shaped W Hotel. Pez Vela serves up classic Paellas and other Mediterranean specialties at its San Sebastià beachside location. For a bird's eye view of the Med, combine with cocktails at Eclipse, the adjacent W Hotel's rooftop bar.

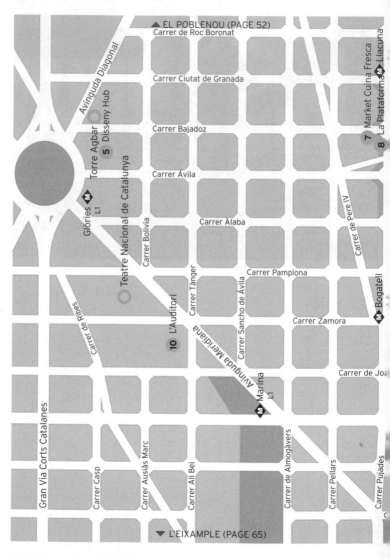

▲ EL POBLENOU (PAGE 52)

Carrer de Roc Boronat

Carrer Ciutat de Granada

Avinguda Diagonal

Torre Agbar

5 Disseny Hub

Carrer Bajadoz

Carrer Ávila

Ⓜ Glóries
L1

Teatre Nacional de Catalunya

Carrer Bolivia

Carrer Álaba

Carrer de Pere IV

7 Market Cuina Fresca

8 La Plataforma ▲ Ⓜ Llacuna

Carrer Pamplona

Carrer Tànger

Carrer Sancho de Ávila

Ⓜ Bogatell

Carrer Zamora

○ L'Auditori

10

Avinguda Meridiana

Carrer de Ribes

Carrer de Joa

Ⓜ Marina
L1

Gran Via Corts Catalanes

Carrer Casp

Carrer Ausiàs Marc

Carrer Ali Bei

Carrer de Almogàvers

Carrer Pellars

Carrer Pujades

▼ L'EIXAMPLE (PAGE 65)

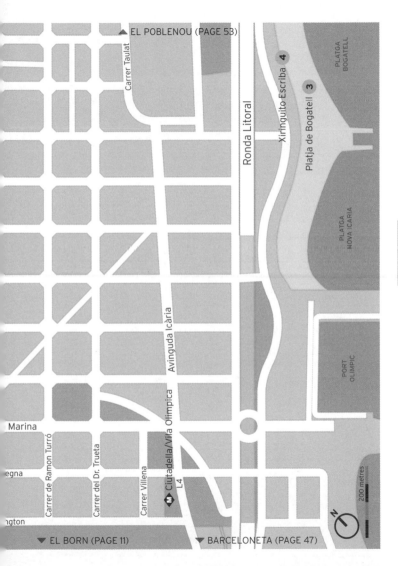

EL POBLENOU (PAGE 53)

Carrer Taulat

Ronda Litoral

Xiringuito Escriba **4**

Platja de Bogatell **3**

PLATGA
BOGATELL

PLATGA
NOVA ICARIA

PORT
OLÍMPIC

Avinguda Icària

Marina

Carrer de Ramon Turró

Carrer del Dr. Trueta

Carrer Villena

egna

Ciutadella/Vila Olímpica
L4

ngton

200 metres

N

EL BORN (PAGE 11)

BARCELONETA (PAGE 47)

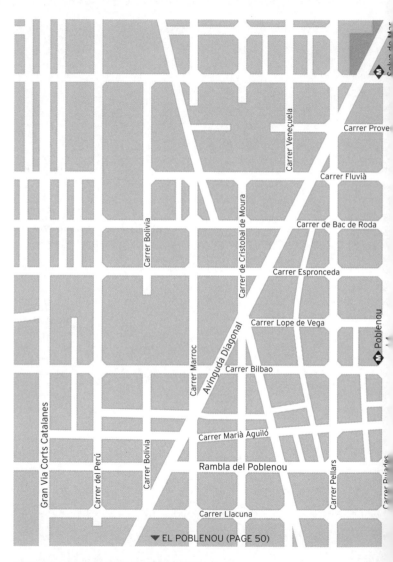

Carrer Venecuela

Carrer Prove

Carrer Fluvià

Carrer de Bac de Roda

Carrer Espronceda

Carrer Lope de Vega

Poblenou

Carrer Bolivia

Carrer de Cristobal de Moura

Carrer Marroc

Avinguda Diagonal

Carrer Bilbao

Gran Via Corts Catalanes

Carrer del Perú

Carrer Bolivia

Carrer Marià Aguiló

Rambla del Poblenou

Carrer Pellars

Carrer Rujades

Carrer Llacuna

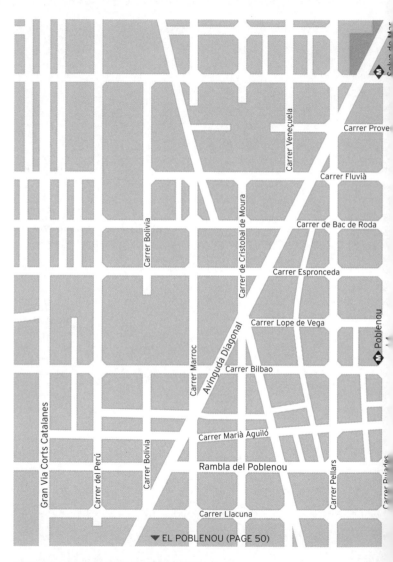

▼ EL POBLENOU (PAGE 50)

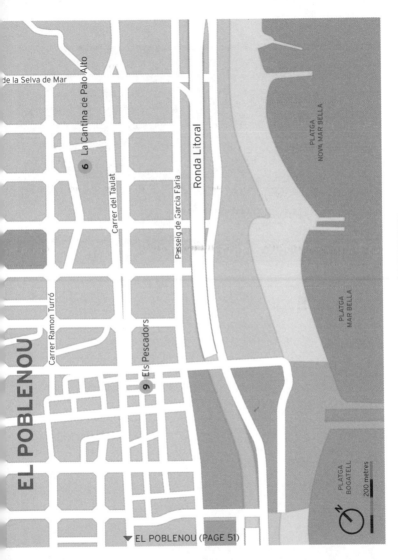

EL POBLENOU

de la Selva de Mar

6 La Cantina de Palo Alto

Carrer del Taulat

Carrer Ramon Turró

Passeig de Garcia Fària

Ronda Litoral

9 Els Pescadors

▼ EL POBLENOU (PAGE 51)

PLATGA NOVA MAR BELLA

PLATGA MAR BELLA

PLATGA BOGATELL

200 metres

Urban Beach

Platja del Bogatell

 Avenida Litoral, between Carrer de Jaume Vincens i Vives and Passatge Llacùna

◆ Llacuna **L4**

Public access.

Two beaches up the coast from the commercial Port Olímpic, Bogatell is arguably the most pleasant of the city's urban beaches. With a couple of relaxed *xiringuitos*, a generous stretch of fine sand and some decent waves lapping the shore, this is a great spot to kick back and forget your cares. Since all of Barcelona's beaches can become crowded during surfing season, Bogatell is especially recommended for a stroll on the warmer days of the low season or in the early morning before the crowds descend.

Beachside Paella

Xiringuito Escriba

 Avenida Litoral, 42
+34 93 221 07 29
xiringuitoescriba.com

◈ Llacuna **L4**

Open daily. Lunch Mon-Thu 1pm-4:30pm, Fri-Sun 1pm-3pm. Dinner Mon-Thu 8pm-11pm, Fri/Sat 8pm-11:30pm.

With an unbeatable location atop Bogatell beach (p54), Xiringuito Escriba offers sizzling and scrumptious *paella* to be devoured directly from the pan with a wooden spoon. Over the colder months, patrons are still made to feel the gentle effects of sun and surf thanks to the restaurant's glasshouse, which offers direct views of the sea. Order a bottle of *cava* and a sumptuously inky *arroz negro* to indulge in some Catalan-style hedonism.

Design Hub

Disseny Hub

5 Plaça de les Glòries, 37
+34 93 309 15 40

dhub-bcn.cat

◈ Llacuna **L4**

Scheduled to fully open in spring 2014. Refer to website for earlier events and exhibitions.

Created by merging the collections of the Museu de les Arts Decoratives, Museu Tèxtil i d'Indumentària, the Gabinete de las Artes Gráficas and the Museu de Ceràmica, the Museo del Diseño de Barcelona, scheduled to open in the spring of 2014, will be an exhibition space dedicated to the culture of the object. The museum will also manage the Casa Bloc's apartment, la Vivienda 1/11, a landmark example of Barcelona's rationalist architecture, open to the public by appointment.

Creative Canteen

La Cantina de Palo Alto

6 Carrer Pellaires 30-38
+34 93 307 09 74

paloaltobcn.org

◆ Selva de Mar L4

Closed Sat/Sun. Open Mon-Fri 8am-noon; 1pm-3.30pm.

La Fundació Palo Alto is made up of nineteen creative studios set within a former industrial space with a lush and beautifully restored courtyard. The foundation's cavernous and ebullient "canteen" is a testament to contemporary Barcelona's creative edge. An excellent seasonal lunch menu changes daily and is as inventive as the work sprouting out of the surrounding studios. Massive communal tables are conducive to inspired conversation igniting across the room.

Market-driven Lunch

Market Cuina Fresca

 Carrer Badajoz, 83
marketcuinafresca.tumblr.com

◈ Llacuna L4

Closed Sat/Sun. Open Mon-Fri 8am-5pm.

As implied in its title, Market Cuina Fresca offers tasty plates composed from the freshest market driven produce the region has to offer. Flavours are expertly combined and each vegetable gleams healthfully on its dish. Market's friendly and casual ambiance is lapped up by the neighbourhood creative set enjoying some excellent home cuisine.

Creative Space

La Plataforma

8 Carrer de Pujades, 99
+34 934 85 65 19
laplataformabcn.com
◈ Llacuna L4
Closed Sat/Sun. Open Mon 11am-3pm; Tue-Fri 10am-2pm, 4pm-8pm.

La Plataforma is an independent art gallery and creative space on the Carrer Pujades, the Poblenou's most innovative stretch. The gallery, which focuses on audiovisual, multimedia and digital art, as well as musical production, blends into a retail outlet carrying art and design related objects, books and children's supplies. Much of the art is created in a studio located upstairs.

That Noble Cod
Els Pescadors

9 Plaça de Prim, 1
+34 932 25 20 18
elspescadors.com

◈ Poblenou **L4**

Open daily. Lunch 1pm-3.45pm.
Dinner 8pm-11.30pm.

A top-notch restaurant specialising in a dazzling array of expertly prepared fish dishes including seven different styles of Bacalau, Els Pescadors merges culinary tradition and contemporary flair. During the warmer months reserve a table at the breezy outdoor patio with views of one of the Poblenou's most charming squares, mid-19th century Plaça de Prim.

Contemporary Classical

L'Auditori

10 Carrer de Lepant, 150
+34 932 47 93 00
auditori.cat
◆ Marina **L1**✖, Monumental **L2**
Daily performances. Refer to website
for program.

Barcelona's premier classical concert
hall and home to the Orquestra
Simfònica de Barcelona since its
establishment in 1999, L'Auditori
offers a multifaceted program of
symphonic, chamber, modern and
choral performances. Down the
street from Jean Nouvel's Torre
Agbar and the up-and-coming
shops and eateries of Poblenou's
Carrer Pujades, L'Auditori's
contemporary feel blends into
the neighbourhood's fresh and
progressive outlook.

L'Eixample

—Modernista Architecture and Contemporary Flavours

The Eixample, literally the "Extension", makes up the bulk of contemporary Barcelona. Based on a 19th century street grid, it is home to the city's famous *modernista* architecture—the Catalan variety of *Art Nouveau*. The most central and oldest parts of the Eixample are the traditional domicile of the Catalan bourgeousie and the site of high quality restaurants, upmarket fashion brands and lawyer and doctor practices.

The plains outside Barcelona's city walls were long off limits for development and consisted primarily of farmland and orchards. This changed in the 19th century when the advent of industrialisation transformed the densely populated city into a squalid hotbed of unrest and disease. The city council held a competition to design Barcelona's extension beyond the city walls, but the Spanish central government instead approved another plan: Ildefons Cerdà ingeniously created octagonal blocks to optimise traffic, sunlight and ventilation. Cerdà had envisioned mixed communities with gardens at their centre, but the city's socio-economic reality soon turned the area around Passeig de Gràcia into corporate offices and entertainment venues. In the central part of the Dreta de l'Eixample (its "right-hand side"), the burgeoning city's bourgeoisie enlisted *modernista* architects to design their homes and professional practices.

The Eixample's lower right fringes are dominated by the textile trade, today an integral part of Barcelona's Chinese community. The Esquerra de l'Eixample (its "left-hand side") is overall more democratic in feel and its architecture more utilitarian. The area's blue-collar northern fringes are the site of Antoni Gaudí's Sagrada Família, slated for completion in 2026.

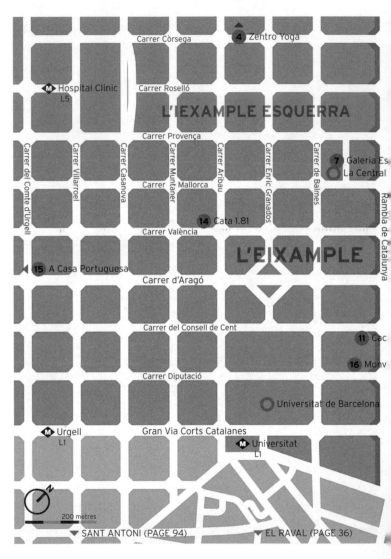

Carrer Còrsega

4 Zentro Yoga

M Hospital Clinic
L5

Carrer Roselló

L'IEXAMPLE ESQUERRA

Carrer Provença

Carrer del Comte d'Urgell

Carrer Villarroel

Carrer Casanova

Carrer Muntaner

Carrer Aribau

Carrer Enric Granados

Carrer de Balmes

Rambla de Catalunya

7 Galeria Es
La Central

Carrer Mallorca

14 Cata 1.81

Carrer València

15 A Casa Portuguesa

L'EIXAMPLE

Carrer d'Aragó

Carrer del Consell de Cent

11 Cac

16 Monv

Carrer Diputació

Universitat de Barcelona

M Urgell
L1

Gran Via Corts Catalanes

M Universitat
L1

N

200 metres

▼ SANT ANTONI (PAGE 94)   ▼ EL RAVAL (PAGE 36)

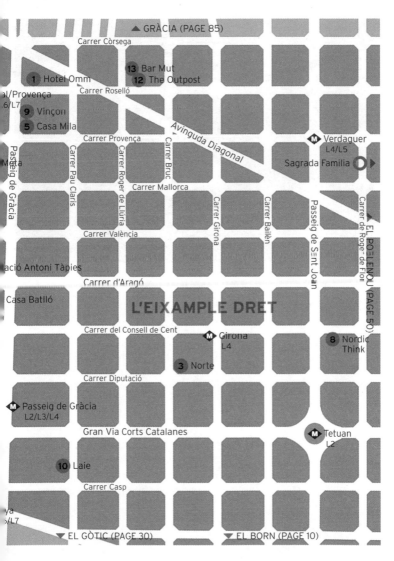

GRÀCIA (PAGE 85)

Carrer Còrsega

1 Hotel Omm

13 Bar Mut
12 The Outpost

Carrer Rosselló

al/Provença
6/L7

9 Vinçon

5 Casa Mila

Avinguda Diagonal

Carrer Provença

Verdaguer
L4/L5

Sagrada Familia

Carrer Pau Claris

Carrer Roger de Llúria

Carrer Bruc

Carrer Mallorca

Carrer Girona

Carrer Bailèn

Passeig de Sant Joan

Carrer de Roger de Flor

EL POBLENOU (PAGE 50)

Passeig de Gràcia

Marta

Carrer València

ació Antoni Tàpies

Carrer d'Aragó

Casa Batlló

L'EIXAMPLE DRET

Carrer del Consell de Cent

Girona
L4

8 Nordic
Think

3 Norte

Carrer Diputació

Passeig de Gràcia
L2/L3/L4

Gran Via Corts Catalanes

Tetuan
L2

10 Laie

Carrer Casp

ya
5/L7

EL GÒTIC (PAGE 30)

EL BORN (PAGE 10)

Uptown Luxury
Hotel Omm

1 Carrer Del Rosselló, 265
+34 934 45 40 00
hotelomm.es

◆ Diagonal/Provença L3 L5 L6 L7
Doubles from €219/night incl. tax

Hotel Omm is the hotel incarnation of Barcelona's gastronomic powerhouse Grupo Tragaluz. Located in a posh Eixample block a stone's throw from the city's main artery, the Passeig de Gràcia, the hotel feels fresh and plush. All rooms are meticulously appointed with natural elements such as parquet flooring and hand-woven rugs. Take advantage of Omm's foodie connections by dining in at in-house restaurant Moo or opt for an evening dip in the rooftop pool before retreating to the Roca bar.

Stunning Apartments

DestinationBCN

2 Throughout the Eixample
+34 935 14 19 50
destinationbcn.com
Apartments from €170/night incl.
tax. €66 cleaning fee/stay.

DestinationBCN offers a string of luxurious self-catering flats throughout the Eixample. Meticulously appointed with a tasteful mix of international design elements from Catalonia, Scandinavia and Italy, Destination BCN takes full advantage of Barcelona's superlative housing stock. Accommodation includes the Principal, a sprawling 1,720 square foot two bedroom three-bathroom Eixample-style apartment complete with interior courtyard, and the Naoko, a contemporary one-bedroom penthouse with wall-to-wall sliding glass doors and a spacious private deck.

Shades of White

Norte

3 Carrer de la Diputació, 321
+34 935 28 76 76
norterestaurante.com

◆ Girona L4, Tetuan L2
Closed Sat/Sun. Open Mon-Fri 8am-
11pm.

A chic and friendly neighbourhood café, Norte specialises in delicious avant-garde tapas and excellent coffee. For breakfast, stop by for some *huevos revueltos* and a *café con leche* at the indoor/outdoor seats flanking the windows and take in the Eixample street life and the café's characteristic white décor.

Urban Yoga

Zentro Yoga

(4) Carrer Aribau, 226
+34 646 22 67 48

zentroyoga.com

◈ Diagonal/Provença L3 L5 L6 L7,
Gràcia L6 L7

Daily classes, refer to website for
schedule. Single class €15

With its vaulted ceilings and cosy
industrial-alpine accents, Zentro
Yoga is at once a haven from the
bustle of urban life and one of
Barcelona's premier venues for
practicing your *asanas*. Founders
Mónica Ponce and Mercedes de la
Rosa were pioneers of the dynamic
vinyasa-style yoga in the city when
they opened their studio almost a
decade ago. Still going strong, the
studio's cosmopolitan atmosphere
and consistently high standards of
instruction make it a standout.

Barcelona Originals

Gaudí Houses

Passeig de Gràcia
+34 932 16 03 06
lapedrera.com; casabatllo.es
◈ Diagonal/Provença **L3** **L5** **L6** **L7**,
Passeig de Gràcia **L2** **L3** **L4**
Casa Milà: Open daily 9am-8pm
(Mar-Oct); 9am-6.30pm (Nov-Feb).
Admission €16.50
Casa Battló: Open daily 9am-9pm.
Admission €20.35

Two of Antoni Gaudi's masterpieces can be found within a few blocks on the fashionable Passeig de Gràcia. The 1904 Casa Batlló (photo p63) is the result of Gaudi's naturalist remodelling of the Batlló family's classical home, adding bone-shaped columns and a *trencadís* broken tiled facade. In contrast, the 1910 Casa Milla (pictured above) was commissioned by a flashy developer/heiress couple. More dominant than playful, it was nicknamed La Pedrera ("the quarry"). The building includes many design novelties, such as a self-supporting stone façade and an underground garage.

Mixed Media

Fundació Antoni Tàpies

6 Carrer d'Aragó, 255
+34 934 87 03 15
fundaciotapies.org

🚇 Passeig de Gràcia **L2** **L3** **L4**,
Diagonal/Provença **L3** **L5** **L6** **L7**
Closed Mon. Open Tue-Sun 10am-7pm. Admission €7.

The Fundaciò Antoni Tapies opened in 1984 in the former Montaner i Simon publishing house building, designed in 1885 by Lluís Domènech i Montaner, the *modernista* architect also responsible for the Palau de la Musica (p25). The building was the first in the Eixample to combine exposed brick and iron in one structure. The foundation regularly exhibits the mixed media work that Tapiès was most famous for, in addition to disseminating modern and contemporary art through shows, lectures and films.

Contemporary Art

Galeria Estrany de la Mota

 Passatge de Mercader, 18
+34 932 15 70 51
estranydelamota.com
◈ Passeig de Gràcia **L2 L3 L4**,
Diagonal/Provença **L3 L5 L6 L7**
Closed Sun/Mon. Open Tue-Fri
10.30am-7pm; Sat 10.30am-2.30pm.
Free admission.

Located on an elegant pedestrianised side street of the Eixample Esquerra, Estrany de la Mota is a cutting edge gallery showing the work of innovative contemporary artists, with a penchant for photography. Ring the doorbell to be granted admittance to the generous basement space a world apart from the ornate streetscape above. If you're in need of a pick-me-up to add exhilaration to inspiration, wander over to the café at La Central's uptown branch just around the corner (see map p64).

Nordic Design

Nordic Think

8 Carrer Consell de Cent, 412
+34 932 456 866
nordicthink.com

◈ Tetuan 🇱2, Girona 🇱4
Closed Sun. Open Mon-Fri 10am-
2pm, 4pm-8pm; Sat 11am-2pm.
Closed July-September.

A touch of Scandinavia by the Med, Nordic Think assembles contemporary Nordic design pieces in a light and cheerful space. Owner Jordi Martin curates a tasteful selection of unique objects and textiles for home, garden and travel, as well as an assortment of children's toys from across the design-driven region.

Design Empire
Vinçon

9 Passeig de Gràcia, 96
+34 932 15 60 50
vincon.com

◈ Diagonal/Provença L3 L5 L6 L7
Closed Sun. Open Mon-Fri 10am-
8.30pm; Sat 10.30am-9pm.

Vinçon is a design emporium
tailored to a design-obsessed city.
Located in a *modernista* palace
towards the upper end of the
Passeig de Gràcia, complete with
gorgeous exterior courtyard,
Vinçon stocks contemporary and
classical design objects from across
the world. The shop's selection of
design and architecture related
books is also excellent.

Coffee and Intellect

Laie

 Carrer Pau Claris, 85
+34 933 02 73 10

laie.es

◆ Passeig de Gràcia **L2 L3 L4**,
Urquinaona **L1 L4**

Closed Sun. Open Mon-Fri 9am-9pm;
Sat 10am-9pm.

A bastion of intellect and culture in the heart of the Eixample, the Laie bookshop-cum-café is a refuge from the city's hustle. Browse the excellent selection of international books and journals before heading upstairs to enjoy a *pincho* with coffee at the well-appointed café. On warmer days, relax on the outdoor patio with a newspaper and a fresh *ensaïmada*, a snail shaped pastry. Laie also boasts a string of cafés in cultural hotspots throughout the city, including an outpost at Gaudí's La Pedrera (p70).

Chocolate Boutique and Café
Cacao Sampaka

11 Carrer del Consell de Cent, 292
+34 932 72 08 33
cacaosampaka.com
◈ Passeig de Gràcia **L2 L3 L4**,
Catalunya **L1 L3 L6 L7**
Closed Sun. Open Mon-Sat 9am-9pm.

If you're looking for your chocolate fix, make for chocolatier Cacao Sampaka's boutique and café in the central Eixample. Though Sampaka has branches further afield, this was the original shop, first opening its doors in the year 2000. Row upon row of delectable single origin artisanally crafted chocolates in various flavours and degrees of intensity line the shop's interior. Proceed to the back café for a chocolate sampler and an intense café solo, or opt for a luxuriously dark *chocolate a la taza* with some feather light *melindros*.

Quality-driven Fashion

The Outpost

(12) Carrer Del Rosselló, 281
+34 934 57 71 37
theoutpostbcn.com

◆ Verdaguer L4 L5, Diagonal/
Provença L3 L5 L6 L7
Closed Sun. Open Mon-Sat 10.30am-
2.30pm, 4.30pm-8.30pm.

This shop is a true outpost for high quality and unusual men's fashion and accessories at the intersection of northern Passeig de Gràcia's retail bling and the central Eixample's *modernista* blocks. Plush interiors by Pilar Libano allow for a luxurious browsing experience, while the expertly curated selection of man-bags, crafted leather belts, wallets and shoes exude easy-going élan. The shop's sumptuous window displays are worthy of a trip in of themselves.

Celebrating Sparkle

Bar Mut

 Carrer Pau Claris, 192
+34 932 17 43 38

barmut.com

◈ Diagonal/Provença L3 L5 L6 L7
Open daily. Mon-Fri 1pm-midnight;
Sat/Sun 11.30am-midnight. Dinner
seatings at 8pm and 10.15pm.

If you fancy a glass of high-end
cava or some top quality Spanish
wine and tapas in a boisterous turn
of the century ambience, Bar Mut
is the place. The bar's location in an
elegant Eixample block sandwiched
between villagey Gràcia and
the whizzy Passeig de Gràcia is
a microcosm of Barcelona street
life. During warmer months, the
outdoor terrace allows patrons to
take in the surrounding *modernista*
architecture, while winter evenings
spent inside exude the celebratory
sparkle inherent in a glass of
bubbly.

Oenological Treat

Cata 1.81

(14) Carrer Valencia, 181
+34 933 23 68 18
cata181.com
◆ Diagonal/Provença **L3** **L5** **L6** **L7**,
Universitat **L1** **L2**
Closed Sun. Open Mon-Sat 7pm-
midnight.

As its name implies, Cata 1.81
specialises in a curated selection
of regional and Spanish wines, but
also takes a fantastic stab at the
Catalan small plates and tapas that
they were made to pair with. A
sophisticated but easygoing space,
Cata is the ideal spot to evade
reality while dipping into innovative
renditions of classic dishes with
wine to match.

Vinho Português

A Casa Portuguesa

15 Carrer Aragó, 111
+34 932 26 25 77
acasaportuguesa.com
◆ Rocafort L1, Entença L5
Open daily. Mon-Sat 1pm-1am; Sun
1pm-8pm.

A fabulous Portuguese wine bar and restaurant, A Casa Portuguesa brings the best of the Douro and Alentejo to the Catalan capital. Enjoy the prime selection of Portuguese wines with pastries and savoury snacks or pop by for an exquisite Bacalhao à Bras if you're after something a bit more substantial. With its exposed brick and eclectic decor, the space is cosy, unpretentious and inviting. A Casa Portuguesa also retails a range of Portuguese wines.

Futuristic Wine

Monvinic

 Carrer de la Diputació, 249
+34 932 72 61 87

monvinic.com

◈ Passeig de Gràcia L2 L3 L4,
Universitat L1 L2

Closed Sat/Sun. Open Mon-Fri 1pm-
11.30pm.

Technology meets oenology at this slick and futuristic wine bar. Taste some of the world's best wines, including exotic selections such as Nyetimber, an English sparkling wine, by the glass at your plush swivel chair. Menus are digital and the space is reminiscent of a cross between a 1970s and a noughties rendition of a luxuriously decked-out space station.

Gràcia

—Urban Hillside Village

Resting on the lower slopes of Barcelona's famous montainous backdrop, Gràcia feels like a small town removed from the rest of the city. Yet at the same time it is the archetypical Barcelona neighbourhood. Its narrow streets and picturesque squares bustle with politically conscious artistic types, Catalan old-timers who have spent their entire lives here, and young families attracted by its village character.

Gràcia dates back to the 17th century when the area was settled by only a few isolated farmhouses and three convents, among which the eponymous Carmelite convent of "Nostra Senyora de Gràcia". The emerging Vila de Gràcia embraced industrialisation and by the mid-19th century had become the most important town to be engulfed by the expanding city of Barcelona.

Gràcia boasts an immense range of independent retail on its high streets, notably Carrer Asturies and Carrer Verdi, but urban village life famously takes place on its squares. Each has its own distinct character: Plaça de la Virreina is known for its charming boutiques, cafés and Romanesque church, while Plaça del Sol teems with Middle Eastern cuisine. Smaller squares further uphill are characterised by their family friendly installations. The neighbourhood's artistic edge has also bestowed it with Barcelona's most comprehensive choice of independent cinematic offerings.

On a steadily steeper track up the hill from Gràcia lies Antoni Gaudi's famous Park Güell (p87). Further up and best reached by its designated funicular, the imposing Tibidabo mountain topped by the Temple de Sagrat Cor, provides stunning views and is visible from almost any point in the city.

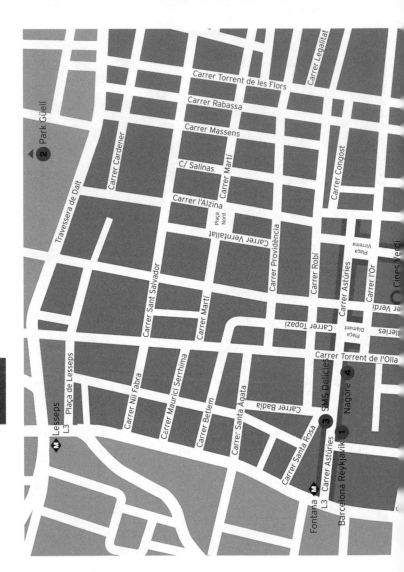

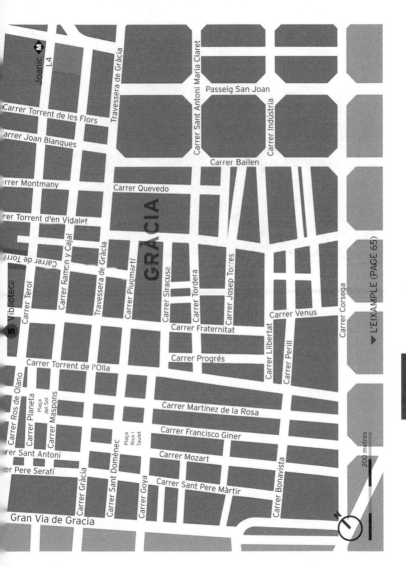

Joanic M L4

Carrer Torrent de les Flors

Carrer Joan Blanques

Travessera de Gràcia

Carrer Sant Antoni Maria Claret

Passeig San Joan

Carrer Indústria

Carrer Bailen

Carrer Montmany

Carrer Quevedo

Carrer Torrent d'en Vidalet

GRÀCIA

Carrer de Torri

Biblioteca

5

Carrer Terol

Carrer Ramon y Cajal

Travessera de Gràcia

Carrer Puigmartí

Carrer Siracusa

Carrer Tordera

Carrer Josep Torres

Carrer Venus

Carrer Fraternitat

Carrer Progrés

Carrer Llibertat

Carrer Perill

Carrer Corsega

▼ L'EIXAMPLE (PAGE 65)

Carrer Torrent de l'Olla

Carrer Ros de Olano

Carrer Planeta

Plaça del Sol

Carrer Maspons

Carrer Martínez de la Rosa

Carrer Francisco Giner

Plaça Rius i Taulet

Carrer Sant Antoni

Carrer Pere Serafí

Carrer Gràcia

Carrer Sant Domènec

Carrer Mozart

Carrer Goya

Carrer Sant Pere Màrtir

Carrer Bonavista

Gran Via de Gracia

200 metres

N

Icelandic Loaves

Barcelona Reykjavik

1. Carrer Astúries, 20
+34 932 37 69 18
barcelonareykjavik.com
◆ Fontana L3
Open daily 10.30am-9.30pm.

Barcelona Reykjavik is the brainchild of Catalan-Icelandic couple David Nelson and Gudrun Margret. An organic bakery with three convivial locations in the city's most charming neighbourhoods (see Born p11 and Raval p36), Reykjavik was borne out of the frustration with the conventional selection of breads available at local *forns*. Focusing on spelt, the ancient and highly digestible form of wheat, Reykjavik produces a high quality traditional style selection of breads, savoury snacks and pastries, including an olive oil dark chocolate chip brioche and luxuriously healthy rendition of *Sachertorte*.

Gaudí Park

Park Güell

2 Uphill from Gràcia
◆ Lesseps ⬛
Open daily 8am-9pm. Free admission.

Set on a rocky hill above Gràcia, the Antoni Gaudí designed Park Güell provides stunning views over the entire city. Commissioned by Count Güell and opened in 1922, the park was originally planned to be the site of an upmarket housing development inspired by the English garden city movement, but only two houses were completed. Gaudí himself moved into one, today the Gaudi House Museum. After Güell's death, his heirs decided to sell the site to the city to make it a public space.

Breakfast your Style

SMS Delicies

3 Carrer d'Astúries, 33
+34 932 17 95 47
smsdelicies.com

◆ Fontana **L3**

Closed Sun. Open Mon-Thu 7.30am-midnight; Fri 7.30am-1.30am; Sat 8.30am-1.30am.

A fun spot to grab breakfast before taking an extensive walk around Gràcia's multiple squares, SMS Delicies offers a delectable assortment of filling treats. Choose from a range of brekkies, from Catalan-style *pan amb tomatquet*, to English-style scrambled eggs and toast, all with *café con leche*, a *zumo* or *batido*. Though breakfast here is a real treat, SMS maintains its jovial atmosphere throughout the day.

Minorcan Sandals

Nagore

 Carrer Asturies, 50
+34 933 68 83 59

nagore.es

◆ Fontana L3

Closed Sun. Open Mon-Sat 10.30am-2pm, 4.30pm-8.30pm.

Menorca based Nagore started producing its unique ecological sandals and shoes in 1983. Building on their success on the craft market circuit, the company expanded to three brick-and-mortar outlets, first in the Balearics and then in Barcelona. Modelled on Minorcan *abarcas* sandals, Nagore goes way beyond the traditional with a glorious array of vegetable tanned colours and sumptuous ergonomic shapes designed to fit like a glove and inspired by the laid-back maritime lifestyle of the Med.

Neighbourhood Wine Bar

Viblioteca

5 Carrer de Verdi, 58
+34 933 68 35 28
viblioteca.com
◆ Fontana **L3**, Joanic **L4**
Open daily. Mon-Sat 6pm-1am; Sun
7pm-midnight. Lunch Sat/Sun 1pm-
4pm.

An intimate and sophisticated
neighbourhood wine bar, Viblioteca
exudes a casually cosmopolitan
ambience. Indulge in the excellent
selection of Spanish wines at the
long and lively bar or pop back to
one of the high tables to sample
some first rate contemporary tapas
with your vino. If you're feeling like
catching an independent film after
drinks, the Verdi Cinemas are just up
the hill (see map p84).

Sant Antoni & Montjuïc

—Blue-Collar World Expo Grounds

The neighborhoods of Sant Antoni and the Poble Sec lie wedged between the Old Town and Montjuïc, a steep hill overlooking Barcelona and its harbour. Divided by Paral·lel avenue, both have maintained much of their traditional blue-collar character and are culturally and socially intertwined with the nearby Raval (p34).

Montjuïc is topped by a 17th century castle that played an important role in the defense, and subjugation, of Barcelona, until it was turned into a museum in 1963. The area owes much of its present-day role as a parkland/tourist sight to the 1929 International Exposition which led to large-scale construction on and around the hill, including the majestic Palau Nacional, which today houses the Museu Nacional d'Art de Catalunya (MNAC), Mies van der Rohe's German national pavilion (p99), and Barcelona's Olympic Stadium, originally intended for an anti-fascist alternative to Berlin's 1936 Olympics.

The Poble Sec, or "dry village", due to the lack of springs in the area, is a narrow strip of dense urbanity on the steep slopes of Montjuïc. It owes its existence to a quirk of history: it sprung up in in the few years after the removal of Barcelona's city walls in 1854, but before plans for the Eixample (p62) had been approved. In contrast, Sant Antoni is laid out over the rigid Eixample grid. It is dominated by the spectacular 1882 Sant Antoni market hall, which primarily served the Raval until Sant Antoni was built up in anticipation of the 1929 International Exposition held nearby. In the interwar years, Paral·lel avenue turned into Barcelona's centre for nightlife, cabarets and social and political innovation, to the extent that a replica of the Moulin Rouge opened in 1910, though its appearance today does not conjure up much of its profligate past.

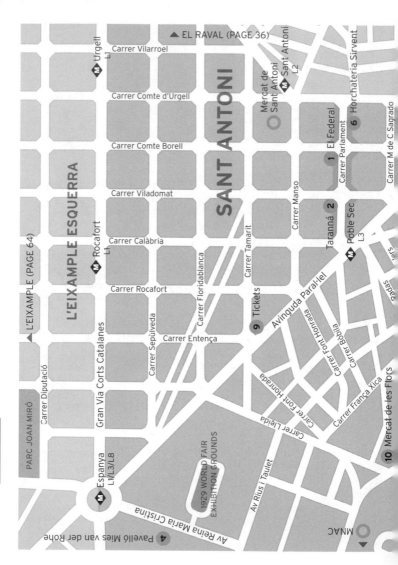

▲ EL RAVAL (PAGE 36)

Carrer Vilarroel

Urgell L1

Carrer Comte d'Urgell

Carrer Comte Borell

Carrer Viladomat

SANT ANTONI

Mercat de Sant Antoni

Sant Antoni L2

Horchateria Sirvent

Carrer M de C Sagrado

6

El Federal

1

Carrer Parlament

L'EIXAMPLE ESQUERRA

Carrer Calàbria

Rocafort L1

Carrer Manso

Carrer Tamarit

Carrer Floridablanca

Carrer Rocafort

Poble Sec L3

Tarannà 2

Carrer Sepúlveda

9 Tickets

Avinguda Paral·lel

Carrer Font Honrada

Carrer Bobila

◀ L'EIXAMPLE (PAGE 64)

Carrer Entença

Carrer Diputació

PARC JOAN MIRÓ

Gran Via Corts Catalanes

Carrer Font Honrada

Carrer Lleida

Carrer Franca Xica

10 Mercat de les Flors

Espanya L1/L3/L8

1929 WORLD FAIR EXHIBITION GROUNDS

Av Rius i Taulet

MNAC

Av Reina Maria Cristina

4 Pavelló Mies van der Rohe

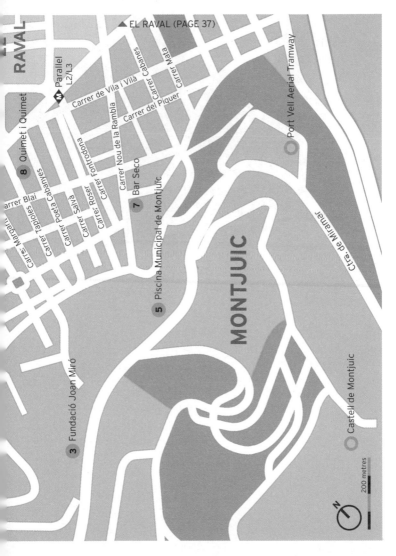

RAVAL

▲ EL RAVAL (PAGE 37)

Ⓜ Parallel L2/L3

Carrer de Vila i Vilà

Carrer Cabanes

Carrer Mata

Carrer del Piquer

Carrer Nou de la Rambla

Carrer Fontrodona

8 Quimet i Quimet

Carrer Margarit

Carrer Blai

Carrer Tapioles

Carrer Poeta Cabanyes

Carrer Salvà

Carrer Roser

7 Bar Seco

Carrer Nou de Montjuïc

3 Fundació Joan Miró

5 Piscina Municipal de Montjuïc

MONTJUIC

Port Vell Aerial Tramway

Ctra. de Miramar

Castell de Montjuic

N

200 metres

SANT ANTONI & MONTJUÏC   PAGE 95

Fancy a Flat White

El Federal

 Carrer Parlament, 39
+34 931 87 36 07
federalcafe.es

◆ Sant Antoni 🄻, Poble Sec 🄻
Open daily. Mon-Thu 8am-midnight;
Fri 8am-1am; Sat 9am-1am; Sun
9am-5.30pm.

El Federal brings a proper Antipodean brunch to the Catalan capital. A cheerful, modern space on a sunny corner of Sant Antoni, this café/restaurant serves up delicious Aussie-style brunches and other healthy dishes. Sit at the ground floor common table to pour over the press of the day with a flat white or head upstairs to the roof deck (complete with lemon tree) for an easy going *tête-à-tête*.

Coffee and Beetroot Cake

Tarannà

2 Carrer de Viladomat, 23
+34 931 06 11 93
tarannacafe.com

◆ Poble Sec L3, Sant Antoni L2
Open daily. Mon 9am-8pm; Tue/Wed
9am-midnight; Thu/Fri 9am-1am; Sat
10am-1am; Sun 10am-5pm.

An attractive bar and café in the
heart of Sant Antoni, Tarannà is
the perfect spot to catch up over
coffee and a slice of vivid purple
beetroot cake or to kick back with
a good glass of wine. Tarannà's
relaxed, sophisticated vibe reflects
the neighbourhood's increasingly
intellectual and creative tendencies.

Catalan Whimsy

Fundaciò Joan Miró

3 Parc de Montjuïc
+34 934 43 94 70
fundaciomiro-bcn.org
◆ Paral·lel L2 L3, up Montjuïc via
furnicular, or Pl Espanya L1 L3 L8
Closed Mon. Open Tue/Wed/Fri/
Sat 10am-7pm (July-September
10am-8pm); Thu 10am-9.30pm; Sun
10am-2.30pm. Admission €11.

Set on the stunning slope of
Montjuïc with views over the city,
the Fundacio Joan Miró houses
the world's most comprehensive
private permanent collection of
the whimsical Catalan artists' work,
as well as a range of temporary
exhibitions striving to introduce
and disseminate the latest
contemporary art in its multiple
representations. Josep Lluís Sert, a
celebrated local architect and friend
of Miró's, designed the museum's
sun drenched rationalist structure
to reflect the spirit of the artist's
work and of the Mediterranean.

Pepo Segura – Fundació Mies van der Rohe

Iconic Architecture

Mies van der Rohe Pavillion

4 Av Francesc Ferrer i Guàrdia, 7
+34 934 23 40 16
miesbcn.com
◆ Pl Espanya **L1** **L3** **L8**
Open daily 10am-8pm.
Admission €5.

Mies van der Rohe was commissioned to design the German Pavilion to represent the new Weimar Germany at the 1929 World Fair. An important building in the history of modern architecture, it introduced such concepts as the free plan to a broad audience. The iconic Barcelona chair was specifically designed for the building. Planned to be temporary, the pavilion was torn down in 1930 but reconstructed from original plans in the 1980s.

A Pool with a View

Piscina Municipal de Montjuïc

 Avinguda de Miramar
+34 934 43 00 46

◆ Paral·lel L2 L3, up Montjuïc via furnicular

Open August only, daily 11am–6.30pm. Admission €6.49

Perhaps the most dramatic public swimming pool in the world, the Montjuïc municipal pool provides stunning panoramic views over the entire city. Built in 1929, the pool hosted events for the 1955 Mediterranean Games and the 1992 Summer Olympics. Today it consists of a diving pool and a 25-metre swimming pool. It is open to the public during the summer months.

Tiger Nut Treat

Horchateria Sirvent

6 Carrer Parlament, 56
+34 934 41 27 20
turronessirvent.com
⊕ Universitat **L1 L2**, Urgell **L1**
Open daily 9am-1am.

Sirvent has an established reputation for excellent handmade *turrón* (nougat) and *horchata*, the refreshing tiger nut drink (both specialties from Valencia province). Founded in 1920 by Xixon native and nougat maker Tomás Sirvent Planelles, the long queues thronging the block leading up to the shop attest to the quality of its products.

Slow Food in the Sun

Bar Seco

 Passeig Del Montjuïc, 74
+34 933 29 63 74

barseco.blogspot.com

◈ Paral·lel L2 L3

Open daily. Mon-Wed 8am-8pm; Thu
8am-1am; Fri 8am-2am; Sat 10am-
2pm; Sun 10am-8pm.
Lunch Mon-Fri 1pm-4pm; Sat 1pm-
5pm; Sun 1pm-6pm.
Dinner Fri-Wed 8pm-midnight; Thu
8pm-11pm.

Located on a sun drenched corner
at the foot of Monjuic, Bar Seco
serves excellent organic brunches
and casual slow food throughout
the day while doubling as a spot
to grab a G&T after the sun goes
down. Sit at the zinc bar beneath
the playfully oversized yellow lamps
to revitalize, then brave the trek up
Montjuic before exploring the Miró
museum (p98) and its stunning
views over the city.

Tapas and Wine

Quimet i Quimet

 Carrer del Poeta Cabanyes, 25
+34 934 42 31 42

◆ Paral·lel L2 L3

Closed Sun. Lunch Mon-Sat noon-4pm. Dinner Mon-Fri 7pm-10.30pm.

A renowned neighbourhood *taberna* and tapas bar, Quimet i Quimet has purveyed a spectrum of tapas and *montaditos* since 1914. Located on one of the Poble Sec's higgledy-piggledy slopes, the tiny space brims with top-notch wine bottles and other epicurean delights. Chef Quim Pérez ensures that the tapas menu remains fresh and innovative, playing on traditional flavours and styles. The space tends to fill out fast, so be prepared to stand for your supper.

Carnavalesque Cuisine

Tickets

 Avinguda Paral·lel, 164
+34 932 92 42 53
ticketsbar.es
◈ Poble Sec ⬛, Rocafort ⬛
Closed Sun. Open Mon-Sat 7pm-11.30pm. Brunch Sat 1pm-3.30pm.

The collaborative brainchild of Albert and Ferran Adriá of El Bulli and restaurateur brothers Juan Carlos, Borja and Pedro Iglesias, Tickets takes the art of tapas to lofty heights in a carnavalesque setting. Divided into six specialized bar sections, each serving distinct dishes reflecting a particular aspect of Barcelona culture, the restaurant is in equal parts theatre and culinary emporium. The open kitchen allows you to catch some of the backstage molecular performance first-hand.

Modern Dance
Mercat de les Flors

10 Carrer del Poeta Cabanyes, 25
+34 934 42 31 42
mercatflors.cat
◆ Poble Sec **L3**, Pl Espanya **L1** **L3** **L8**
Regular performances. Refer to
website for schedule. Admission
from €8.

Housed in the magnificent former
Palace of Agriculture, which was
built for the 1929 World Expo, the
Mercat de les Flors is Barcelona's
mecca for modern dance.
Renowned theatre director Peter
Brook produced his own plays here
in 1983 and convinced the then
mayor of Barcelona Pasqual Margall
to renovate the space. The glorious
12-metre dome overhanging
the entrance foyer is the work of
Majorcan artist Miquel Barceló.

Essentials

Airport Transfer
Barcelona's El Prat Airport has among the best ground transport links of any major European airport. A taxi ride to Plaça Catalunya in the heart of the city will cost around €25-30 and take approximately 20 minutes. There are usually plenty of taxis available at Arrivals at any time of day.

Terminal 2 is the terminus of line R2 of Barcelona's Rodalies commuter train network. Trains depart every 30 minutes to stations throughout central Barcelona. The travel time to central Passeig de Gràcia is 26 minutes and a single ticket costs €2.35. Zone 1 integrated travel cards are valid on this service.

Aerobús (aerobusbcn.com, +34 902 100 104) provides a bus service between both terminals and Plaça Catalunya. Throughout the day buses depart every 5 minutes from Terminal 1 and every 10 minutes from Terminal 2. The travel time is 35 minutes and a single ticket costs €5.90. Travel cards are not valid.

An expansive overhaul of the airport's rail connections is underway. In the near future, both terminals will have dedicated stations with both Metro (L9) and Rodalies services. The Spanish AVE high-speed train network will also have a new station near the airport.

Taxis
Barcelona taxis are plentiful and relatively inexpensive. Most inner city journeys take less than 15 minutes and usually cost under €10. There are also relatively few delays during rush hour as taxis can resort to bus lanes on congestion prone commuter routes. In all but rare cases drivers are competent and fares transparent. Many, though not all, Barcelona taxis accept credit cards. It is recommended to ask the driver before the start of the journey if credit cards are accepted.

Public Transport
First opened in 1924, the Barcelona Metro, operated by TMB, is clean, fast

and efficient. Trains operate from 5am to midnight (Sun-Thu), until 2am on Fridays and 24 hours on Saturday nights. Trains depart every 3-4 minutes depending on the line and time of day. Delays are very rare, to the degree that departure times are displayed in seconds.

A single ticket costs €2. In addition there are a number of integrated travel cards that can be used on all Barcelona public transport. A carnet of 10 rides (T-10) costs €9.80, a day pass (T-Dia) €7.25 and a monthly pass (T-Mes) €52.75. There are also 2 to 5-day travel cards. All metro stations and the airport are in fare zone 1.

Suburban train services operated by Rodalies and FGC provide easy and convenient access directly from the city centre to the beaches and wine regions around Barcelona. Note that FGC also somewhat confusingly operates Metro lines L6, L7 and L8. See p112 for the Metro map.

Tipping
Spain, like other southern European countries, does not have an elaborate tipping culture. Tips are not expected in taxis or cafés, though considered polite if more than usual attention was required. In restaurants, round up to the nearest euro or two, and tip around 5% at higher-end establishments.

Safety
Barcelona is generally a safe and prosperous city. Given its high population density and Spain's late night culture, there is a fair amount of foot traffic at most times of day. That being said, the medieval *Ciutat Vella* (Old Town), and in particular the Raval, is made up of a maze of tiny alleyways that don't get much sunlight even during the day, making them prone to petty theft.

Index

A

Accommodation. *See* Hotel
Airport Transfer — 106
Architecture
  Barcelona Cathedral — 28
  Gaudí Houses — 70
  Mies van der Rohe Pavillion — 99
  Modernista — 62
  Park Güell — 87
  Sagrada Família — 62
  Santa Maria del Mar — 8
  Torre Agbar — 44

B

Bar. *See* Wine bar
  Bar Mut — 78
  Bar Seco — 102
  Eclipse (W Hotel) — 49
  Juanra Falces — 26
  Roca (Hotel Omm) — 66
Barceloneta — 44
Barri Gòtic — 28
Beaches
  Barceloneta — 44
  Platja del Bogatell — 54
Beauty
  Henna Morena — 17
Books
  La Central — 41
  Laie — 75
  Mutt — 16
Born — 8

Brunch
  Bar Lobo — 42
  Bar Seco — 102
  El Federal — 96
  Norte — 68
  Picnic — 14
  SMS Delicies — 88

C

Café
  Bar Seco — 102
  Norte — 68
  SMS Delicies — 88
  Tarannà — 97
Call, El — 28
Concerts. *See* Music

D

Dance
  Mercat de les Flors — 105
Design
  Disseny Hub — 56
  Nordic Think — 73
  Vinçon — 74

E

Eixample — 62

F

Fashion
  El Born — 8
  La Clinique — 18
  Nagore — 89

The Outpost	77	Mercat de Sant Antoni	92
Food		Metro	106
Barcelona Reykjavik	86	Metro Map	112
Cacao Sampaka	76	Montjuic	92
Casa Gispert	19	Museum	
Horchateria Sirvent	101	CCCB	40

G

Gallery. *See also* Museum
Círculo del Arte	15
Fundació Antoni Tàpies	71
Galeria Estrany de la Mota	72
La Plataforma	59
Mutt	16

Gaudí
Gaudí Houses	70
Park Güell	87
Sagrada Família	62

Gràcia | 82

Fundació Joan Miró | 98
MACBA | 34
MNAC | 92

Music
L'Auditori	61
Palau de la Musica	25

P

Paral·lel | 92
Parks
Montjuic	92
Parc de la Ciutadella	13
Park Güell	87

Poblenou | 44
Poble Sec | 92
Pool
CEM sports centre	13
Piscina Municipal de Montjuic	100

H

Hotel
Casa Camper	38
DestinationBCN	67
Grand Hotel Central	12
Hotel Omm	66

L

Las Ramblas | 28

M

Market
Mercat de la Boqueria | 39

R

Restaurant
Antipodean
El Federal	96
Picnic	14

Beachside
Pez Vela	49
Sal Café	48

Xiringuito Escriba 55
Fusion
Salero 21
Iberian
Bar Lobo 42
Comerç 24 23
La Cantina de Palo Alto 57
Market Cuina Fresca 58
Saboc 24
Italian
Bacaro 43
Japanese
Koy Shunka 32
Seafood
Els Pescadors 60
Xiringuito Escriba 55
Tapas
Cal Pep 22
Cata 1.81 79
Quimet i Quimet 103
Tickets 104

S

Safety 107
Sant Antoni 92

T

Tapas. *See* Restaurant: Tapas
Taxis 106
Tibidabo 82
Tipping 107

V

Views
Montjuic 92
Park Güell 87
Piscina Municipal de Montjuic 100
Port Vell Aerial Tramway 44
Tibidabo 82
W Hotel (Eclipse bar) 49

W

Wine
Vila Viniteca 20
Wine bar. *See also* Bar
A Casa Portuguesa 80
Monvinic 81
Viblioteca 90

Y

Yoga
Zentro Yoga 69

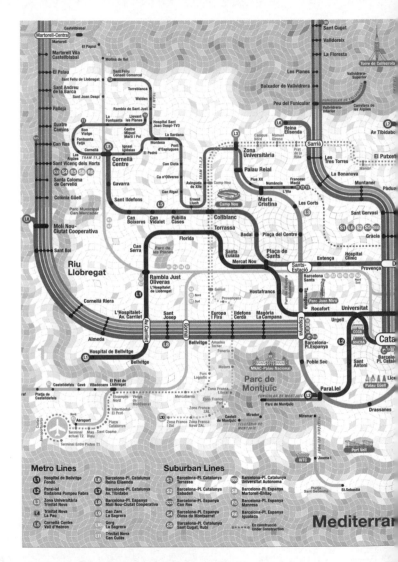

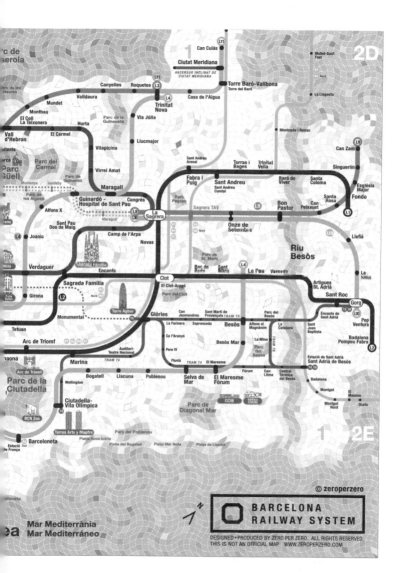

Credits

Published by Analogue Media, LLC
244 5th Avenue, Suite 2446, New York, NY 10001, United States

Edited by Alana Stone
Layout & Production by Stefan Horn

For more information about the Analogue Guides series, or to find out about availability and purchase information, please visit analogueguides.com

First Edition 2013
ISBN: 978-0-9838585-3-9

Every effort has been made to ensure the accuracy of the information in this publication. However, some details are subject to change. The publisher cannot accept responsibility for any loss, injury, inconvenience, or other consequences arising from the use of this book.

Typefaces: Neutraface 2, Myriad Pro and Interstate
Paper: Munken Lynx

Printed in Barcelona by Agpograf, S.A.

Analogue Media would like to thank all contributing venues, designers, manufacturers, agencies and photographers for their kind permission to reproduce their work in this book.

Barcelona Railway System map © zeroperzero
Cover design by Dustin Wallace
Proofread by John Leisure

Photography credits: all images credited to the listed venues unless stated otherwise. (9) Stefan Horn (14) Stefan Horn (17) Lili Bonmati (19/20) Stefan Horn (21) Roberto Ruiz (22) Ferran Nadeu (24) Stefan Horn (25) Antoni Bofill. Palau de la Música Catalana archive (26/29) Stefan Horn (32) Pedro Cortacans (35) Stefan Horn (38) Copyright: Camper (39) Stefan Horn (40) © CCCB, José Antonio Soria, 2013-01-22 (41/43/45) Stefan Horn (49) Olga Planas (54) Marina Valdor (56/57/58) Stefan Horn (61) Joan Altés (63) Stefan Horn (66) Olga Planas (68) Calaca V. (69) Stefan Horn (70) Lisa A / Shutterstock.com (72) Jean-Marc Buslamonto (73) Carme Masià (77) Josep Piella (79) Meritxell Arjalaguer (80/83/86) Stefan Horn (87) Stanislaw Tokarski / Shutterstock.com (88/93) Stefan Horn (96) Lucia Carretero (98) Foto Juan Morejón. © Fundació Joan Miró (99) Pepo Segura - Fundació Mies van der Rohe (100/101/102/103) Stefan Horn (104) Moises Torne (105) Pau Fabregat.

About the Series

—A Modern Take on Simple Elegance

Analogue Guides is a series of curated city guidebooks featuring high quality, unique, low key venues—distilled through the lens of the neighbourhood.

Each neighbourhood is complemented by a concise set of sophisticated listings, including restaurants, cafés, bars, hotels and serendipitous finds, all illustrated with photographs. The listings are supplemented by custom designed, user-friendly maps to facilitate navigation of the cityscape. Venues featured in the guides score high on a number of factors, including locally sourced food, tasteful design, a sophisticated and relaxed atmosphere and independent ownership.

Analogue Guides are designed to complement the internet during pre-travel preparation and smartphones for on-the-ground research. Premium photography and a select choice of venues provide an ideal starting point for pre-travel inspiration. At your destination, the guides serve as portable manuals with detailed neighbourhood maps and clear directions.

The result: a compact, efficient, effervescent manual celebrating the ingenuity of the contemporary metropolis.